2008

PIANO · VOCAL · CHORDS

W9-CTB-913

COUNTRY SUPERSTARS
SHEET MUSIC

PlayList

SONGS THAT MADE THE YEAR!

Alfred Publishing Co., Inc.
16320 Roscoe Blvd., Suite 100
P.O. Box 10003
Van Nuys, CA 91410-0003
alfred.com

ISBN-10: 0-7390-5743-X
ISBN-13: 978-0-7390-5743-8

CONTENTS

JUST GOT STARTED LOVIN' YOU

Words and Music by
D. VINCENT WILLIAMS, JIM FEMINO
and JAMES OTTO

Moderately slow ♩ = 92

Verses 1 & 2:

1. You don't have to go now, hon-ey, call 'em, tell 'em you won't be in to - day.___
2. What's the point in fight-in' what we're feel-in'? We both know we'll nev-er win.___

Ba - by, there ain't noth-in' at the of - fice so im - por-tant it can't
Ain't this what we're miss-in'? Let's just stop all this re - sist-in' and give

D.S. %

Repeat ad lib. and fade

ALL SUMMER LONG

Words and Music by MATTHEW SHAFER, R.J. RITCHIE,
WARREN ZEVON, LEROY MARINELL, WADDY WACHTEL,
ED KING, GARY ROSSINGTON and RONNIE VAN ZANT

1. It was Nine-teen eight-y nine,___ my thoughts were short,___ my hair was long,___ caught ___ some-where be-tween___ a boy___ and man.___

14

sum-mer long.___ Sing-in' "Sweet_ Home Al - a - bam - a"___ all sum - mer long.___

Ah.___

Ah.___

Freely

ALL-AMERICAN GIRL

Words and Music by
CARRIE UNDERWOOD, KELLEY LOVELACE
and ASHLEY GORLEY

1. Since the day they got mar- ried, he'd been pray- in' for a
2. Six- teen short years lat- er, she was fall- in' for the

All-American Girl - 6 - 1

A BABY CHANGES EVERYTHING

Words and Music by
TIM NICHOLS, CRAIG WISEMAN
and K.K. WISEMAN

Verse 7:

7. My whole life was turned a - round. I was lost, but

now I'm found. A ba - by chang - es ev - 'ry - thing.

A

ba - by chang - es ev - 'ry - thing.

BOB THAT HEAD

Words and Music by
NEIL THRASHER, GARY LEVOX
and MICHAEL DULANEY

Drop D tuning:
⑥ = D ③ = G
⑤ = A ② = B
④ = D ① = E

Verse 1:

Bob that__ head,_____ *come on!* Bob that head._____

Bob that__ head,_____ *woo!*

Verse 2:

2. Hot girl wants a ride, climbs up in - side. Feel-in' that rhy - thm right a - long with him.

Now he's cruis - in', don't wan-na lose__ it. Loop a-round Son - ic and right back__ on it.

HOLLER BACK

Words and Music by
TIM JAMES and STOKES NIELSON

Moderate country rock ♩ = 84

1. I got a

Holler Back - 7 - 1

Verse:

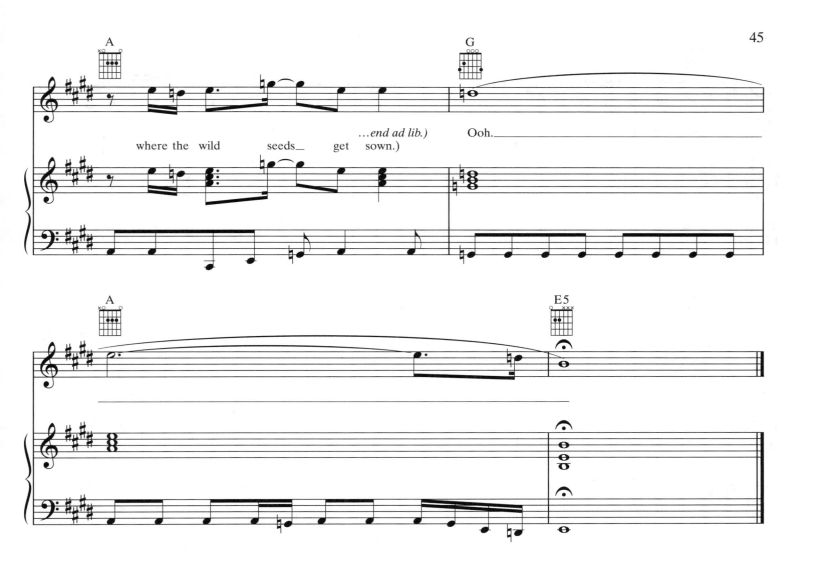

where the wild seeds get sown.) ...end ad lib.) Ooh.

Verse 2:
Take a left off the Interstate,
Go ten miles,
Take a right on Farm Road 99
And just roll 'til the blacktop ends.
You'll see Mary Jo rockin' that front porch swing,
Bikini top and them cut-off jeans,
And that's where hillbilly heaven begins.
Ah, she'll pour you some of that cherry wine.
Boy, you're guaranteed to have yourself
One hell of a time.
In that holler back...
(To Chorus:)

DO YOU BELIEVE ME NOW

Words and Music by
TIM JOHNSON, DAVE PAHANISH
and JOE WEST

Moderately slow ♩ = 88

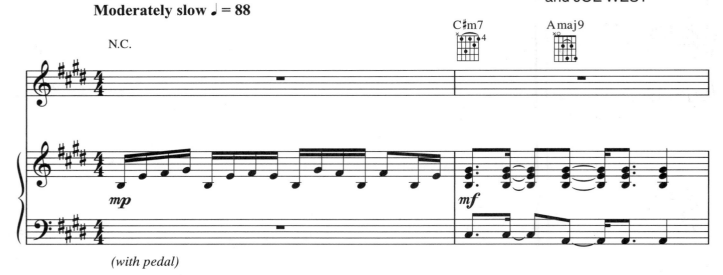

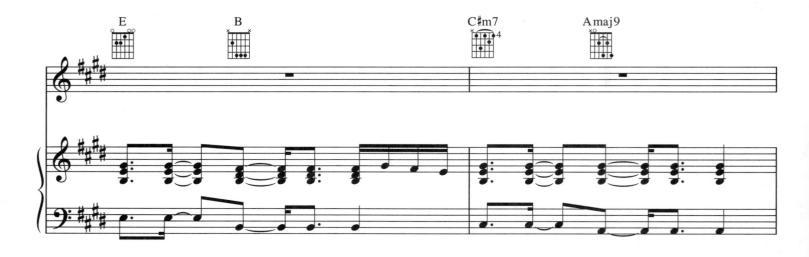

(with pedal)

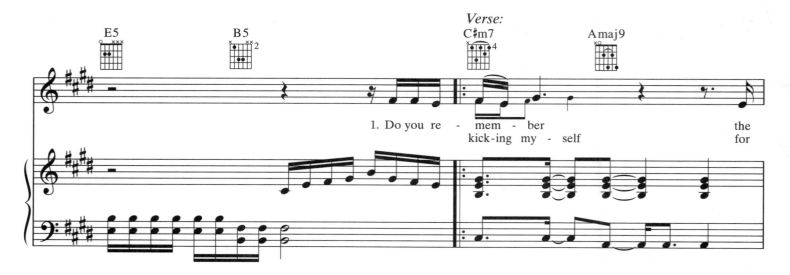

Verse:

1. Do you re - mem - ber   the
kick-ing my - self   for

EVERY OTHER WEEKEND

Words and Music by
CONNIE HARRINGTON and SKIP EWING

Verse:

Reba:

1. Ev - 'ry oth - er Fri - day___ it's toys and clothes in back - packs. Is
2. *See additional lyrics*

ev - 'ry - bod - y in___ o - kay? Let's go___ see Dad.___

Same time, in the same spot, cor - ner of the same___ old___ park - ing lot.

Every Other Weekend - 7 - 1

week - end._____

week - end._____

a tempo

rit.

G 2

A/C#   D(9)

Verse 2:
(Reba:)
Every other Saturday,
First thing in the morning,
I turn the TV on to make the quiet go away.
I know why, but I don't know why
We ever let this happen.
Fallin' for forever was a big mistake.
There's so much not to do and all day not do it in
Every other weekend.

(Kenny:)
Every other Sunday,
I empty out my backseat
While my children hug their mother in the parking lot.
We don't touch, we don't talk much,
Maybe goodbye to each other
As she drives away with every piece of heart I've got.
I re-convince myself we did the right thing
Every other weekend.
(To Chorus:)

EVERYBODY

Words and Music by
RICHARD MARX and KEITH URBAN

1. So, here you are__ now, no-where to turn.__ It's just the same old yes-ter-day.

And you made a prom-ise to your-self that you were nev-er gon-na

Chorus:

GOOD FRIEND AND A GLASS OF WINE

Words and Music by
LEANN RIMES, DARRELL BROWN
and BLAIR DALY

Verse:

1. Who died___ and crowned___ me ev - 'ry - bod - y's ev - 'ry - thing?___
2. I don't need___ to jet off___ on no va - ca - tion for a week.___

I'm e - ven bust -ing my butt___ through the week - end.___
I'd be hap - py to have___ a hap - py ho - ur.___

By the time___ I get home,___ there's not an ounce of san - i - ty.___ Be - tween the
When I'm tired___ and I'm fried,___ it get's me right back on my feet.___ Yeah, an - y

dogs, my mom - ma's calls,___ is it a - gainst the law   for me to get what I need?
kind of red or white,___ a lit - tle sis - ter - time,   it's ev - 'ry smart girl's se - cret.

cresc.

Chorus:

A good friend and a glass of wine,_____ some-one to say it's gon-na be al-right._____

A good friend and a glass of wine,_____ a lit-tle pick-me-up to get me through the night._____

We talk trash and we laugh and cry._____ That kind of ther-a-py mon-ey can't buy._____

Ev-'ry now and then, ev-'ry now and then, ev-'ry girl needs__ a good friend and a glass of wine.__

Good Friend and a Glass of Wine - 6 - 4

Chorus:

HOME

Words and Music by
MICHAEL BUBLÉ, ALAN CHANG
and AMY FOSTER

Home - 6 - 1

I've had my run, and, ba-by, I'm done. I'm com-ing back

home. Let me go home. It-'ll be al-

Freely

right, I'll be home to-night. I'm com-ing back home.

HOW LONG

Words and Music by
J. D. SOUTHER

Moderately fast ♩ = 138

Verse 1:

1. Like a blue - bird_____ with his heart_____ re - moved_____ – lone - ly as a train_____ I've run just as far___

How Long - 8 - 1

How___ long, how___ long? Rock your - self to sleep___

Verse 3:

3. Ev - ery - bod - y feels___ all right,_ you know I heard some_ poor fool say___
(Ooh,_____ some - bod - y.___

Ev-ery-one is out__ there_ on the loose_____ Well, I

wish I lived__ in the land of fools___ and no one knew my name_

But what you get is not___ quite what you

Chorus:

choose._ Tell me How__ long, how__ long–

I STILL MISS YOU

Gtr. tuned down 1/2 step:
⑥ = Eb   ③ = Gb
⑤ = Ab   ② = Bb
④ = Db   ① = Eb

Words and Music by
TIM NICHOLS, KEITH ANDERSON
and JASON SELLERS

Moderately slow ♩ = 84

Guitar ➔ E5   A2   E5   A2
Piano ➔ Eb5   Ab2   Eb5   Ab2

mf

1. I've changed the pre-

Verse:
E5 / Eb5   A2 / Ab2

sets in my truck,___ so those old___ songs don't sneak___ up,___ but they still find___
'til you were gone___ how man-y pag-es you were___ on. Well, it nev-er___

E5 / Eb5   A2 / Ab2

___ me and re-mind___ me. Yeah, you___ come back___ that eas-y. Try res-tau-rants___
___ ends, I keep turn-in' them, line af-ter line,___ you're there___ a-gain. Well, I don't___

JUST A DREAM

Words and Music by
HILLARY LINDSEY, STEVE McEWAN
and GORDIE SAMPSON

Moderately slow ♩ = 72

1. It was

(with pedal)

Verse:

two weeks af-ter the day___ she turned___ eigh-teen,___ all___ dressed___ in white,___
preach-er man said,"Let us bow___ our heads___ and pray.___ Lord, please lift his soul___

go - in' to the church that night.___ She had his
and heal this hurt."___ Then the

Just a Dream - 6 - 1

This can't be hap-pen-ing to me._____ This is just____ a dream.

2. The _____ This is just_____ a dream._____

Oh,_____

ba-by, why'd you leave_ me? Why'd you have to go?___ I was count-in' on for-ev - er, now____

LAST NAME

Gtr. tuned down 1/2 step:
⑥ = E♭   ③ = G♭
⑤ = A♭   ② = B♭
④ = D♭   ① = E♭

**Words and Music by
CARRIE UNDERWOOD, HILLARY LINDSEY
and LUKE LAIRD**

Moderately slow country rock ♩ = 80

Verses 1 & 2:

1. Last night, I got served a lit-tle bit too much of that poi-son, ba-by.
2. We left the club right a-round three o'-clock in the morn-ing. His

Last night, I did things I'm not proud of, and I got a lit-tle cra-zy.
Pin- to sit-tin' there in the park-ing lot, well, it should-'ve been a warn-ing.

LET IT GO

Music and Lyrics by
WILLIAM C. LUTHER, AIMEE MAYO
and TOM DOUGLAS

1. I've been

caught side - ways, out here on the cross - roads,
2. Skel - e - tons and ghosts are hid - ing in the shad - ows,

Let It Go - 5 - 1

Oh,___ whoa,___ oh,___ yeah.___

LOVE DON'T LIVE HERE

Lady Antebellum

Words and Music by
DAVID WESLEY HAYWOOD,
CHARLES KELLEY and HILLARY SCOTT

Love Don't Live Here - 7 - 1

Chorus:

LIFE IN A NORTHERN TOWN

Words and Music by
NICK LAIRD-CLOWES
and GILBERT GABRIEL

LOOKIN' FOR A GOOD TIME

Words and Music by
CHARLES KELLEY, DAVE HAYWOOD,
HILLARY SCOTT and KEITH FOLLESE

Hey, whatcha drinkin', baby?

Male:

1. Girl, you're beau-

Verse:

ti - ful,_____ you're 'bout near per - fect,_____ but I

(2.)_____ hard week,_____ do - ing this nine to five. And you're

Lookin' for a Good Time - 6 - 1

*Female lead vocal only 1st time.
Male harmony (in cues) added 2nd time.

PRAYING FOR TIME

Words and Music by
GEORGE MICHAEL

1. These are the days of the o - pen hand._____ They will not be the
2. This is the year of the emp - ty hand._____ Oh, you hold on to what you

last. Look a - round, now.___ These are the days___ of the beg - gars and the choos-
can, and char - i - ty is a coat you wear___ twice a year.___

ers. This is the year of the hun - gry man,_____ whose place is in___ the
These are the days of the guilt - y man,_____ your tel - e - vi - sion takes a stand,___

Praying for Time - 4 - 1

PUT A GIRL IN IT

Words and Music by
BEN HAYSLIP, DALLAS DAVIDSON
and RHETT AKINS

Verse:

1. You can buy you a brand - new truck,
2. You can buy a boat and a shin - y set of skis, have some

chrome it all out,___ jack it way up.___ You can
fun in the sun,___ float a - round in the breeze.___

Bridge:

(Inst. solo ad lib....

...end solo) You can write you a coun-try song.___

The D J___ won't put___ it on.___ They won't dance or

RED UMBRELLA

Words and Music by
AIMEE MAYO, CHRIS LINDSEY,
BRETT WARREN and BRAD WARREN

it ain't gon-na drown_ me. Af - ter all, I'm gon-na be o - kay,_ so let it

1. rain.

2. You can rain._ Oh,_

___ let it rain._ (Rain.) Let it fall. I'm

Verse 2:
You can wear your sorrow like an old raincoat,
You can save your tears in a bottle made of gold.
But the glitter on the sidewalk always shines,
Yeah, even God needs to cry sometimes.

Pre-chorus 2:
Your love is like a red umbrella,
Always there to make me better.
When my broken dreams
Are fallin' from the sky.
(To Chorus:)

MAYBE SHE'LL GET LONELY

Words and Music by
JAMIE PAULIN, JEREMY STOVER
and JOHN KENNEDY

ROLLIN' WITH THE FLOW

Words and Music by
JERRY HAYES

sins._____

3. Some might be call-in' me a bum,

but I'm still out__ here hav-in' fun._____

And Je-sus loves me, yes, I

know,_____

so I keep on roll-in' with the flow.

While guys my age are rais-in'

Bridge:

STRONGER WOMAN

Words and Music by
MARV GREEN and
JEWEL KILCHER

Stronger Woman - 5 - 1

Coda

stron - ger — wom-an, a stron - ger wom - an, there's a stron - ger — wom-an, a

Sung freely

stron - ger wom - an in me,

stron - ger wom - an ____ in me. ____

Verse 2:
The light bulbs buzz, I get up,
Head to my drawer.
Wish there was more I could say,
Another fairy tale fades to grey.
I've lived on hope, like a child,
Walking that mile, faking that smile,
All the while, wishing my heart had wings.
Well, from now on, I'm gonna be
The kind of woman I'd want my daughter to be.
(To Chorus:)

THAT SONG IN MY HEAD

Words and Music by
WENDELL MOBLEY, JIM COLLINS
and TONI MARTIN

That Song in My Head - 5 - 1

D.S. % al Coda

⊕ *Coda*

Verse 3:
I said, "How 'bout an autograph for ya, your biggest fan?"
You wrote your name and your number in the palm of my hand.
My heart and that big bass speaker were thumpin' away.
And I've had that song in my head all day.
(To Chorus:)

THINGS THAT NEVER CROSS A MAN'S MIND

Words and Music by
WYNN VARBLE, DONALD POYTHRESS
and TIM JOHNSON

Moderately ♩ = 120

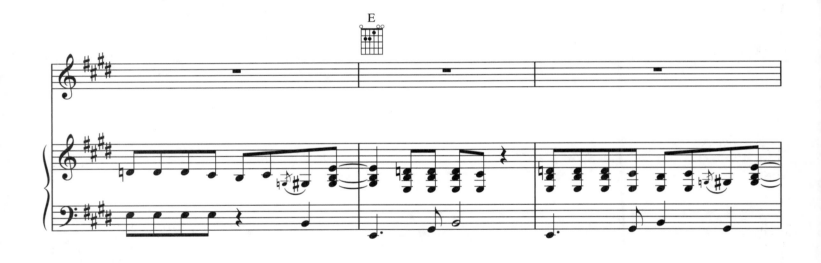

Verse 1:

1. I need to go__ shop-ping; these

Things That Never Cross a Man's Mind - 5 - 1

shoes are all___ wrong.___ Just look in my clos - et; not a thing to put on.___ I

won - der how these jeans___ make me look from be - hind?_____ Things that nev - er cross a

man's_____ mind.___

2. Let's

𝄋 *Verses 2 & 3:*

turn off the T V; now can't we just___ talk?___ Let's lay here and cud - dle 'til we

3. *See additional lyrics*

Verse 3:
Her lips are too red,
Her skirt is too tight,
Her legs are too long,
And her heels are too high.
Boy, she looks like the marryin' kind.
Things that never cross a man's mind.
(To Chorus 2:)

Chorus 3:
I feel a little bloated;
Think I'm fixin' to starve.
That movie was good 'cept for the violent parts.
Brad Pitt is sexy;
Why did he change his hair?
I knew him and Jenny never had a prayer.
These curtains clash with the carpet;
The color scheme is a crime.
Things that never cross a man's mind.

WAITIN' ON A WOMAN

Words and Music by
WYNN VARBLE and DON SAMPSON

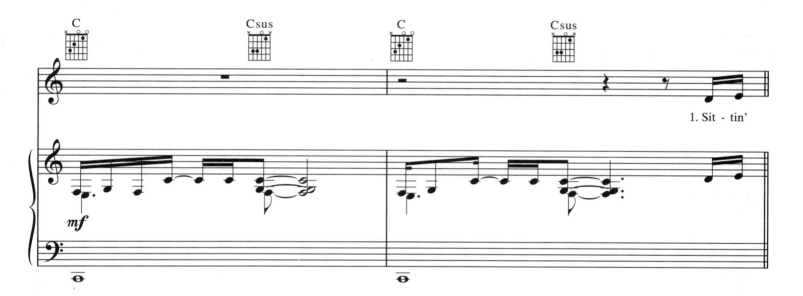

Waitin' on a Woman - 5 - 1

wom-an."

2. He said, "The wom-an."

D.S. 𝄋 al Coda

3. "I've